Beyond Handshakes:

Building Business Relationships in a Digital World

by Hannah Miller

Dear Esteemed Reader,

Thank you immensely for choosing this book to join your collection. We imagine that you've already embarked on an exploration of ideas within these pages, and we couldn't be happier about it!

Now, if you find yourself chuckling, pondering, or even debating with the words in front of you, we'd absolutely love to hear about it. If you can spare a few moments to pen down your thoughts in a review, we would be as delighted as a dictionary on a spelling bee!

An Amazon review would be excellent - but hey, we're far from picky. Whether it's a scribble on the back of a grocery list, a tweet, or even a message in a bottle (though that might take a while to reach us), your feedback is gold.

Writing a review might not be as fun as a spontaneous dance-off, but we promise it'll bring grins to our faces, warmth to our hearts, and incredibly valuable insights to future readers.

With Gratitude,

Bo Bennett, PhD
Publisher
Archieboy Holdings, LLC.

Table of Contents

Preface

Welcome to "Beyond Handshakes: Building Business Relationships in a Digital World". This book is an enlightening expedition into the captivating, often challenging, domain of networking in our contemporary digital age. Each page aims to support you, the modern, tech-savvy professional, as you venture out to form, foster, and finesse your business connections online.

We commence our journey with Chapter 1, exploring the brand-new age of networking, where we'll delve into the concept of digital handshakes and lay down a roadmap for the journey ahead. Next, in Part I, we traverse the evolution of networking in Chapter 2, tracking our path from firm physical handshakes to the ubiquity of hashtags. Chapter 3 uncovers the ever-changing digital landscape, including the impact of social media and the surge of remote and digital-first workplaces.

In Part II, we direct our focus to creating business relationships. From making lasting first impressions to the etiquettes of online networking, Chapters 4 and 5 break down the foundations of building an online presence and initiating authentic connections. We discuss the benefits of professional platforms like LinkedIn and the subtle art of digital conversation.

Transitioning to Part III, we delve into developing these connections into enduring relationships. Chapter 6 is devoted to nurturing online relationships through regular interaction, engagement, and leveraging digital tools. But with growth comes challenges; Chapter 7 offers insights into managing digital fatigue, balancing professionalism and personality online, and ensuring privacy and security in the virtual sphere.

As we advance into Part IV, we concentrate on maintaining and maximizing these relationships. Chapter 8 advises on how to sustain engagement over time and offers tips on personalizing your interactions. We further delve into transforming these connections into valuable collaborations in Chapter 9, including real-world case studies of successful digital collaborations.

Finally, in Chapter 10, we glance into the future of business relationships, pondering over the evolving networking landscape and how one might adapt to upcoming digital shifts.

Throughout your journey with this book, may you find knowledge, inspiration, and practical advice that propels your digital networking to new heights. Let's venture into the enthralling world beyond handshakes, together.

Introduction

Welcome to "Beyond Handshakes: Building Business Relationships in a Digital World," where we embark on an exploration of modern networking and the tools that make it possible. We start by charting the new age of networking, defining what digital handshakes entail in the world of instant messages, likes, and retweets. A roadmap of this book will provide a clear path through the labyrinth of digital networking. We'll delve into the history and influence of technology on business relationships, and navigate through the vibrant landscape of social media and emerging digital platforms. From making the right first impressions online to overcoming challenges unique to the digital realm, you'll learn how to develop, nurture, and maintain business relationships. Finally, we'll gaze into the future, examining upcoming shifts in the digital world and preparing you to adapt and thrive amidst change. Strap in, we're about to dive headfirst into a world where connectivity is only a click away.

The New Age of Networking

In the heart of this digital revolution lies a powerful tool— Networking. No longer confined to the four walls of conference rooms or the restrictive borders of countries, networking has undergone a digital metamorphosis, making the world a smaller and more interconnected place.

In this new age of networking, geographical boundaries have blurred, replaced by borderless digital platforms. These platforms enable you to connect with people from any part of the world, at any time, and from the comfort of your own home. Whether it's a budding entrepreneur in Silicon Valley or an experienced business magnate in Shanghai, all are just a click away. You could be sitting in your living room in Sydney, yet be a part of an engaging business discussion in London. Such is the marvel of digital connectivity.

Yet, with this new platform of networking comes new rules. The transition from in-person interactions to a screen-mediated dialogue poses unique challenges. Conveying your charisma or the firmness of your handshake is no longer viable. Your new business card is your digital profile—be it on LinkedIn, Twitter, or an industry-specific networking site. Your digital profile, your posts, your comments, your shares, and your likes—all contribute to the image you present to the digital world.

Adaptability and relevance have become key to thriving in this landscape. Staying abreast with the latest trends, leveraging popular hashtags, and tapping into trending conversations—these are just some of the strategies that have proved effective in enhancing visibility and engagement in the digital world.

Of course, the rapid pace of this digital age does not diminish the importance of building genuine, meaningful connections. In fact, authenticity becomes more important than ever in an environment where facades are easy to construct. Your sincerity, trustworthiness, and professional credibility must shine through the pixels of your profile and the words of your messages.

Networking, in its core essence, is still about building relationships. It's about finding common ground, fostering mutual respect, and cultivating a sense of camaraderie and cooperation. These principles hold just as true in the digital realm as they do offline. The medium may have changed, but the heart of networking remains the same.

However, it's not all about taking—giving back is just as important. The most successful networkers are those who strive to provide value to others, be it in the form of knowledge, opportunities, or support. In a world where information is abundant and readily available, the currency of networking is no longer just who you know, but what value you can provide.

In the upcoming chapters, we'll dive deep into the intricacies of digital networking. We'll look at how you can build a compelling online presence, make authentic connections, and navigate the challenges unique to the digital realm. With insights from industry experts, real-world examples, and actionable tips, we aim to equip you with the tools and knowledge to thrive in this new age of networking.

So, let's embark on this journey together. It's time to explore and conquer the dynamic world of digital networking. With every connection you make, remember, you're not just building a network, but weaving a global tapestry of diverse ideas, perspectives, and opportunities. Welcome to the new age of networking—beyond handshakes.

Digital Handshakes: An Overview

Navigating the digital networking landscape is akin to being in a bustling, constantly evolving metropolis. In this bustling cityscape, the handshake has found a new avatar - the digital handshake. This is a metaphor for the first impressions, connections, and engagement we initiate in the digital world. Digital handshakes aren't defined by physical touch, but rather by the clink of connection notifications and the welcoming messages exchanged online.

Your digital handshake starts the moment someone encounters your name online. It could be a potential employer looking at your LinkedIn profile, a potential business partner coming across your blog post, or even a peer responding to your comment on a professional forum. The way you present yourself online, the professionalism and sincerity in your interactions, and the value you bring to digital conversations - these factors come together to form your digital handshake.

But, how is a digital handshake different from an in-person one? It's primarily about reach and permanence. While a traditional handshake is momentary and limited to a specific time and place, a digital handshake can reach across continents and leave a lasting impression. It enables you to make a mark and establish your brand in a space where thousands of conversations and interactions are happening simultaneously.

The first point of contact in digital networking is often a well-crafted online profile. Like a stylish business card, it serves as a concise yet comprehensive introduction to who you are and what you do. The importance of investing time and effort into creating a compelling online profile cannot be overstated, as it is often the first step towards making a positive digital handshake.

Then comes the follow-through. Just as in real life, where a good handshake is often followed by engaging conversation, in the digital world too, a good profile needs to be supplemented by active participation in online discussions, sharing insightful content, and initiating meaningful interactions.

Maintaining professionalism while projecting your unique personality is the delicate balance to strike in the world of digital handshakes. The casualness associated with social media platforms might tempt you to let your hair down, but remember, a digital handshake is often the prelude to professional relationships. A dose of personal touch certainly makes the interaction more relatable, but professionalism should be the undertone of your digital conduct.

Beyond mere contact, the digital handshake is also about consent and mutual interest. Unlike an unsolicited email or an intrusive advertisement, a digital handshake happens when both parties show an active interest in initiating a conversation. This mutual consent makes the digital handshake a powerful tool for creating authentic and meaningful business relationships.

A digital handshake is an ongoing process. Each interaction, each shared piece of content, each insightful comment adds to the firmness of your handshake. It's about not just creating impressions, but also about maintaining those impressions over time. As we proceed further into this book, we'll delve deeper into the art and science of mastering digital handshakes—be it for job hunting, building professional connections, or creating business opportunities.

So, let's gear up to decode the complexities, navigate the challenges, and unleash the immense potential of digital handshakes. After all, every tweet, post, like, share, comment, or message could be a handshake that opens doors to incredible opportunities in this boundless digital world.

The Book's Roadmap

Stepping into the digital realm can be daunting. There are myriad platforms to navigate, ever-evolving trends to keep up with, and new rules of engagement to learn. But fear not, this book is your trusty compass, ready to guide you through the fascinating journey of building business relationships in this digital era.

The upcoming chapters of this book are carefully curated and sequenced to take you through a comprehensive, step-by-step exploration of digital networking. Like a well-planned road trip, our journey starts with understanding the landscape, followed by learning the essentials for the journey, overcoming challenges along the way, and, finally, reaching our destination.

Part I: The Digital Revolution, is akin to understanding the roadmap before embarking on a journey. We start with a brief history of networking in Chapter 2 to appreciate how far we've come - from traditional handshakes to digital ones, and the influence of technology on business relationships. In Chapter 3, we take a deep dive into the present digital landscape, exploring the effect of social media, emerging digital platforms, and the rise of remote and digital-first workplaces.

In Part II: Creating Business Relationships, we shift gears to practical skills and strategies for digital networking. In Chapter 4, we discuss how to make powerful first impressions online and utilize various platforms for networking. Chapter 5 focuses on creating authentic connections online, emphasizing the etiquettes of online networking, trust-building, and the art of digital conversation.

As we venture into Part III: Developing Business Relationships, we tackle the nuanced aspects of nurturing online relationships. Chapter 6 focuses on strategies for regular interaction and engagement, the use of collaborative digital tools, and the role of webinars and virtual meetings. In Chapter 7, we address the potential challenges in online networking - managing digital fatigue, balancing professionalism and personality, and ensuring privacy and security.

The final stretch of our journey, Part IV: Maintaining Business Relationships, revolves around sustaining these relationships in the fast-paced digital world. In Chapter 8, we explore techniques to maintain engagement over time, personalizing interactions, and dealing with changes in digital trends. In Chapter 9, we learn how to turn these connections into collaborations and look at case studies of successful digital collaborations.

Our journey culminates with a peek into the future in Chapter 10, where we discuss the evolving networking landscape and how to adapt to future digital shifts. And just like the satisfying conclusion to any journey, we end with some closing remarks and an appendix to answer any lingering questions you might have.

And so, with this roadmap in hand, you're ready to embark on an insightful, empowering, and transformative journey towards mastering the art of building business relationships in a digital world. Let's hit the road!

PART I:
THE DIGITAL REVOLUTION

Chapter 1:
A Brief History of Networking

We're about to embark on a journey through time. This chapter navigates through the fascinating evolution of networking, tracing the steps from traditional face-to-face interactions to the complex and nuanced digital exchanges of today. We will explore how networking has transformed from the era of handshakes and business cards to a world dominated by hashtags and social media platforms. Then, we will delve into the profound ways technology has influenced business relationships, shaping and molding them into what they are today. Understanding this history provides us with invaluable insight into our current networking environment and offers us a unique perspective on its future trajectory. So, let's get started and explore the remarkable saga of networking.

From Handshakes to Hashtags

Once upon a time, networking was all about face-to-face interactions. The look in someone's eyes, the inflection of their voice, and of course, the all-important firm grip of a handshake. These were the symbols of a potential business relationship, an unspoken agreement of trust, respect, and mutual benefits.

Fast-forward to the dawn of the 21st century, and we see the dawn of a new age of networking - the age of digital communication. Social media platforms, initially created for casual interactions and friendships, began to reshape the world of networking. LinkedIn, Facebook, Twitter, and a whole array of other platforms ushered in an era where networking wasn't limited to the confines of offices, conferences, or luncheons.

The hashtag - a humble symbol used in a plethora of fields, particularly in information technology, found new life in this digital world. A once overlooked symbol on your keyboard, the hashtag (#), morphed into a powerful tool, revolutionizing the way we communicate and connect online. Chris Messina, a former Google employee, pioneered this transformation in 2007 when he proposed the use of hashtags on Twitter to group related content.

Now, let's take a moment to appreciate how a simple symbol like a hashtag can create global communities. Think about trending hashtags like #MotivationMonday, where people from all over the world share inspiring stories and advice to start the week off right, or #ClimateChange, which has united global voices calling for environmental action.

But like any significant change, this evolution from handshakes to hashtags has come with its challenges. One of the significant hurdles of digital communication is its lack of physicality and the nuances of in-person interaction. There's no body language or tone of voice to interpret, leading to potential misunderstandings. Besides, the vast expanse of the digital space can be overwhelming.

However, these hurdles have not hampered the progress of digital networking. If anything, they have propelled innovators and users alike to create and adapt new ways of building relationships online. The hashtag remains a potent tool in this sphere, a beacon that draws people together based on shared interests and ideas.

Moreover, the hashtag's power extends beyond its ability to aggregate content or start conversations. It's a symbol of inclusion, a way for individuals and businesses to align themselves with causes, events, or movements. By using a hashtag, you're not just joining a conversation; you're joining a community, signaling your membership, and asserting your place within it.

Let's also consider the reach and accessibility the hashtag has introduced to networking. A hashtag can trend globally, opening doors to conversations and connections across continents. In this context, a hashtag is an open invitation - you're just a hashtag away from joining a worldwide community.

Despite the shift from physical to digital, it's important to remember the fundamental principles of networking - trust, respect, and mutual benefit. While the medium has changed, these principles remain as relevant as ever. We must strive to maintain these values in our digital interactions.

Think of the hashtag as our new handshake, our way of reaching out and establishing a connection. It's the modern way of indicating your interest in a conversation, a topic, or a cause. It's our symbol of engagement in this digital age.

By embracing the hashtag, we embrace a world of limitless connections, shared experiences, and collective wisdom. We connect not just with the people we know or the people within our geographical boundaries, but with a global community of diverse individuals. So, dive in, use that hashtag, and see where this journey of digital networking takes you.

The Influence of Technology on Business Relationships

As we've explored, technology, especially social media, has dramatically changed the face of networking. But let's delve deeper and consider the broader influence of technology on business relationships.

Technology has fundamentally reshaped the nature of business interactions. Once upon a time, building business relationships meant meeting in person, phone calls, and exchanging business cards. However, with the advent of technology, particularly digital platforms, we've witnessed a seismic shift in the way these relationships form and flourish.

First, let's examine the immediacy that technology provides. The instantaneous nature of online communication has accelerated the pace of establishing and maintaining business relationships. Whether it's a quick tweet to a potential collaborator or an email to a client across the globe, technology enables us to communicate effectively and swiftly.

The second way technology has influenced business relationships is through accessibility. Today, you're not limited by geographical boundaries or time zones. A business relationship is now possible between a freelancer in Bali and a startup in Berlin, or a consultant in Sydney and a client in New York. The world is at your fingertips, quite literally.

Along with increasing accessibility, technology also provides scalability. Through online platforms and digital tools, businesses can now communicate with a vast audience. Whether it's a brand announcing a new product on Instagram, a company conducting a webinar, or a CEO writing a post on LinkedIn, technology provides a way to interact with a massive audience simultaneously.

Fourth, technology has given rise to a new degree of personalization. Using AI and machine learning algorithms, businesses can now tailor their interactions with customers, improving the customer experience and fostering stronger relationships. Whether it's personalized email campaigns, customized shopping experiences, or targeted ads, personalization is a game-changer in business relationships.

Moreover, technology has enhanced transparency in business relationships. With abundant information available online, customers can easily access and assess a company's track record, values, and reputation. This transparency can bolster trust in business relationships, but it also means businesses must consistently uphold their commitment to authenticity and integrity.

Now, it's important to understand that while technology has brought incredible benefits, it's not without its challenges. The digital landscape has its pitfalls - issues of privacy, cybersecurity, and misinformation, to name a few. Plus, the efficiency and ease of digital communication sometimes may come at the cost of the human touch and personal connection.

One significant challenge is maintaining the balance between efficiency and personalization. Automation can boost efficiency, but it's crucial not to lose the personal touch in business relationships. After all, behind every email, tweet, or direct message, there's a human being, not just a potential business lead.

The influence of technology on business relationships is far-reaching and profound. As digital natives navigating this terrain, it's crucial to leverage technology to build, enhance, and sustain business relationships. However, as we do so, let's not forget the essence of business relationships – mutual respect, trust, and benefit. It's not just about the tech; it's about people. So, as you navigate this digital landscape, remember to make technology your tool, not your master. Harness it to serve your relationships, not to replace them.

Chapter 2: Understanding the Digital Landscape

We've set the stage on the influence of technology in business relationships. Now, it's time to pull back the curtain and reveal the digital landscape in all its complexity and dynamism. This chapter will help you comprehend the ever-evolving world of social media, introduce you to emerging digital platforms, and guide you through the rapid rise of remote and digital-first workplaces. As you traverse this landscape, you'll learn to navigate its highs and lows, turning the digital revolution into your ultimate networking tool. Strap in and get ready to delve into the heart of our modern, interconnected world.

The Social Media Effect

It's impossible to downplay the significant role social media plays in today's interconnected world. These platforms, which seemed like mere entertainment apps in their infancy, have now grown into powerful networking and marketing tools.

Social media platforms such as Facebook, Twitter, Instagram, and LinkedIn have transformed our communication styles and habits. Unlike traditional networking, social media allows us to connect with anyone, anytime, anywhere. This unprecedented accessibility has dissolved geographic borders and time zones, opening up infinite networking possibilities.

On social media, individuals and businesses alike have the ability to build their brand identity and persona. With a carefully curated profile and well-planned posts, businesses can create their online presence and attract a like-minded audience. Similarly, individuals can showcase their skills, achievements, and personality traits to potential employers, clients, or partners.

The way we communicate has also fundamentally changed. Social media enables real-time interaction, creating a sense of immediacy and intimacy. No longer do we have to wait for responses via post or email; a direct message on Instagram or a tweet on Twitter can garner instantaneous replies. This expeditious communication fosters faster relationship-building and collaboration.

But it's not just about the speed and ease of communication. Social media brings an element of personalization to networking. By providing insights into a person's interests, activities, and ideologies, it offers a sneak peek into their lives. This level of transparency and intimacy was previously unattainable, making it a game-changer for relationship-building.

However, social media's impact isn't solely positive. With constant connectivity comes the risk of information overload and privacy breaches. An innocent post can quickly spiral into a controversy if not handled with sensitivity and tact. Balancing the act of being open yet professional is a challenge one must master to harness social media's power effectively.

Social media has also created an expectation for businesses and individuals to be always available. This can lead to burnout and stress, blurring the lines between work and personal life. Maintaining digital wellbeing while utilizing these platforms for networking is a crucial aspect that we must keep in mind.

Furthermore, the rapid pace of social media can be daunting. Trends come and go in a blink of an eye, and staying relevant requires constant adaptation and creativity. The cost of failing to keep up with these trends can be high, leading to missed opportunities and lost connections.

In conclusion, the social media effect is a double-edged sword. It has revolutionized business networking, opening up numerous possibilities, yet it also poses challenges that need to be skillfully navigated. The next sections will delve into how you can tackle these challenges and make the most out of your social media networking journey.

Emerging Digital Platforms

With social media's undeniable presence, we've experienced a surge in digital platforms designed to cater to specific networking needs. Beyond Facebook, Twitter, LinkedIn, and Instagram, there are numerous emerging platforms that are reshaping the digital networking landscape. This section will discuss these emerging platforms and their unique strengths.

In recent years, a new class of networking platforms has emerged, shifting focus from the masses to niche communities. These platforms cater to particular professions, industries, or interests, providing a more targeted networking experience. For instance, AngelList caters to startups, while Behance and Dribbble are popular among designers. Utilizing such platforms offers the opportunity to connect with like-minded individuals and share industry-specific content.

Next, we've seen the advent of audio-only platforms, the most famous being Clubhouse. With Clubhouse, users join virtual rooms and listen to conversations happening in real-time. This platform mimics the experience of attending a conference or a networking event, with the added advantage of joining from anywhere. Other platforms, like Twitter Spaces and Discord, are also leveraging the popularity of audio-based networking.

Another trend on the rise is the use of platforms that capitalize on short-form video content. TikTok, leading the charge, has transformed the way we consume information. Its algorithm's ability to push user-generated content to vast audiences has made it a great platform for personal branding and business networking. TikTok's popularity has led other platforms like Instagram (Reels) and YouTube (Shorts) to introduce similar features.

Decentralized platforms, powered by blockchain technology, are also making their mark. They offer enhanced security, privacy, and user control, appealing to a segment of users who prioritize these features. Sites like Minds and Hive represent this new wave of social networking platforms.

One cannot discuss emerging digital platforms without mentioning VR (Virtual Reality) and AR (Augmented Reality) platforms. While still in their early stages, platforms like Facebook's Horizon Workrooms are offering immersive virtual meeting spaces. They have the potential to take digital networking to an entirely new level by providing a near-physical networking experience.

Last but not least, career development platforms, like Coursera and LinkedIn Learning, also offer networking opportunities. They facilitate connections with peers and experts in the field, offer mentorship opportunities, and help showcase your skills to potential employers or clients.

While leveraging these platforms, remember that each has its unique environment and user expectations. Understanding these nuances and adapting your networking approach accordingly is vital to successful relationships. So, explore these platforms, identify those that align with your goals and preferences, and take your digital networking to the next level.

However, as with all digital interactions, there are inherent challenges, like privacy concerns, information overload, and maintaining authenticity, which will be discussed in subsequent chapters. The key is to harness the advantages of these emerging platforms while skillfully navigating their potential pitfalls. It's about balance – balancing exploration with focus, personalization with privacy, and being on-trend with authenticity.

The Rise of Remote and Digital-first Workplaces

Welcome to the age of remote work and digital-first workplaces. Recent developments have made it abundantly clear that the future of work is less about location and more about connectivity. In this section, we will unpack how this shift to remote and digital-first environments impacts networking, collaboration, and the establishment of business relationships.

The onset of remote work has reshaped our understanding of networking. With the walls of the office dissolving, work and networking are no longer confined to a single geographic location. For individuals, this means the ability to collaborate with professionals from around the world, creating opportunities for global networking that once seemed unimaginable. This shift has also made business relationships more flexible and dynamic, but it has also necessitated that we rethink how we connect and communicate.

Remote work has made digital platforms the primary venue for communication and collaboration. Video conferencing tools like Zoom and Google Meet have become staples of the business world. Beyond meetings, these tools are also used for virtual networking events, webinars, and online training sessions, providing a multitude of ways to engage with colleagues, peers, and thought leaders.

Collaboration tools have also gained significant traction. Tools like Slack, Asana, and Trello are widely used for project management, team communication, and collaboration in remote and digital-first workplaces. Their chat-based interfaces not only aid in task management but also foster casual interactions and camaraderie that are integral to building strong business relationships.

Moreover, the rise of digital-first workplaces has amplified the importance of creating a robust online presence. With the physical office becoming less prominent, your digital profile becomes your representative. This calls for a well-crafted LinkedIn profile, an active presence on relevant digital platforms, and a consistent portrayal of your professional identity.

The shift towards remote and digital-first workplaces has also highlighted the need for individuals and organizations to prioritize digital literacy. Knowing how to navigate various digital platforms, understanding digital etiquette, and being able to communicate effectively online are all now critical skills. Developing these skills can give you a competitive edge and ensure that you are able to participate fully in the digital networking landscape.

However, while the rise of remote and digital-first workplaces brings exciting opportunities, it also presents unique challenges. The blurring of work-life boundaries, the lack of face-to-face interactions, and the risk of digital fatigue are all significant concerns that need to be addressed. Navigating these challenges effectively is key to building and maintaining strong business relationships in the new work paradigm.

As we delve deeper into the age of remote and digital-first workplaces, it's clear that this shift is not just a trend, but a fundamental change in how we work and network. Understanding this landscape, and adapting to it, is the first step in thriving in the new digital business world. As always, the goal remains to forge meaningful connections and foster relationships that fuel personal and professional growth.

PART II: CREATING BUSINESS RELATIONSHIPS

Chapter 3:
First Impressions in the Digital Age

We've all heard the saying: "You never get a second chance to make a first impression." That holds just as true in the digital world as it does in face-to-face interactions. In this chapter, we're turning our focus to how you present yourself online and how you can use different platforms to start building relationships that matter. We'll start with the basics of building a strong online presence, move onto the art of utilizing social media for professional networking, and then dive into leveraging professional platforms, with a special emphasis on LinkedIn. This journey is designed to ensure you make impactful first impressions that pave the way for meaningful connections in the digital age.

Building an Online Presence

Just as we present ourselves physically through our attire, body language, and manners, we present ourselves digitally through our online presence. It's essential to understand that your online presence is more than just a virtual business card. It's your digital persona, a holistic representation of who you are, what you stand for, and how you deliver value to your peers and potential business associates.

Let's start with the basics: what exactly does an online presence entail? Primarily, it involves your digital footprints across the web: your social media profiles, your blog posts or publications, your website, and any comments or reviews you've made online. All these fragments come together to form a picture of who you are online.

The first key to building an effective online presence is consistency. Your digital persona needs to align with your actual persona. This alignment is crucial because when people feel the same energy from your online presence as they do when they meet you in person, it creates a sense of authenticity and trust. Therefore, strive to present your values, your vision, and your vibe consistently across different platforms.

Second, attention to detail is vital. Make sure all your social media profiles and your website are filled out completely, and everything is up-to-date. It might seem like a minor thing, but having a high-quality profile picture, a well-written bio, and a professional header image can make a significant difference. These are often the first things people see when they visit your profile, so make sure they represent you well.

Third, become a thought leader in your field. You can do this by sharing valuable content that helps your audience solve their problems or achieve their goals. This could be blog posts, videos, infographics, or even a podcast. The type of content you share will depend on your industry and your personal preferences. But the key is to consistently deliver value.

The fourth point is to engage with others. It's not enough to just post content and disappear. Respond to comments, share other people's content, and engage in conversations. This not only makes you more visible but also builds relationships and encourages people to interact with you.

Lastly, remember that building an online presence is a marathon, not a sprint. It takes time, patience, and consistency. But the effort is worth it. A strong online presence can help you establish your brand, build relationships, and even open up new opportunities.

While social media is a critical piece of your online presence, remember that it's just a piece. We'll delve into the art of utilizing these platforms for professional networking in the next section. As for now, consider your online presence the cornerstone of your digital networking journey, a foundation upon which all your online relationships will be built.

Utilizing Social Media for Professional Networking

Social media has morphed from a fun distraction into a powerful tool for building professional relationships. Your digital presence on social media platforms acts as an extension of your brand and offers a vibrant, interactive environment for networking. But to make the most out of it, it's crucial to have a nuanced understanding of the different platforms and how they can be leveraged for networking.

Begin with identifying the right platforms for your goals. LinkedIn might seem like the default choice—and it often is for most professionals. However, Twitter, Instagram, and Facebook also have robust communities and can facilitate networking, depending on your industry. So take some time to analyze where your potential connections hang out online and mark your presence there.

Once you've chosen the right platforms, cultivate your profiles with care. Your profile is your digital handshake, your first impression. Remember to use a professional-looking profile picture, craft a compelling bio that clearly states who you are and what you do, and share relevant content that enhances your credibility.

Content sharing is one of the major pillars of social media networking. A thoughtfully curated content strategy can position you as a knowledgeable and credible professional. Whether you share industry news, insightful articles, your original content, or valuable resources, ensure they are tailored to the interests of your network and consistently align with your professional brand.

However, networking isn't just about broadcasting your content; it's a two-way street. Engage with the content shared by your connections. Commenting with your insights on others' posts not only puts you on their radar but also demonstrates your expertise to a wider audience. Plus, it creates opportunities for meaningful conversations that can lead to deeper connections.

Following industry influencers, joining relevant groups, and participating in discussions can also enhance your visibility. On platforms like LinkedIn and Facebook, there are numerous groups for virtually every profession or interest. These groups can be an excellent source of knowledge, offer opportunities to engage with like-minded individuals, and position yourself as an active member of your professional community.

Networking events haven't disappeared in the digital age; they've merely transformed. Live video sessions, webinars, Twitter chats, Instagram Live, and LinkedIn events are the new-age networking events. Participate actively, ask questions, share insights, and you'll notice your network growing steadily.

Another significant aspect is direct messaging. While it can seem daunting initially, sending a personalized message to someone you'd like to connect with can be a powerful networking tool. Be respectful, mention common interests or connections, and articulate why you wish to connect. Keep it friendly and professional, and you might be surprised by the positive responses.

Remember, networking isn't about collecting connections like trophies. It's about building relationships. Always strive for quality over quantity. Ten meaningful relationships with people who value your expertise and are willing to vouch for you can be far more valuable than hundreds of connections who barely know you.

Remember to manage your time on social media wisely. It's easy to get lost in the endless scroll of updates, but mindful usage can help you focus on your networking goals without letting it take over your life. Set aside specific blocks of time for your social media networking activities, and stick to them.

Lastly, be patient and persistent. Building a professional network on social media doesn't happen overnight. It requires consistent effort, patience, and authenticity. But the benefits—access to opportunities, knowledge exchange, partnerships, and even friendships—make it all worthwhile.

In the next section, we'll take a closer look at the key player in professional networking platforms, LinkedIn, and dive into strategies for leveraging it for networking and beyond. But for now, remember that social media is a powerful tool in your networking arsenal. Learn to wield it with skill, and it can open doors to countless opportunities.

Connecting through Professional Platforms: LinkedIn and Beyond

When it comes to digital professional networking, LinkedIn is the undisputed king. With over 700 million users, LinkedIn offers an enormous pool of professionals across a multitude of industries. But LinkedIn is far from the only player in the game. There are numerous other professional networking platforms that have emerged, each with their unique features and benefits.

Let's begin with LinkedIn, the heavyweight champion. LinkedIn is a powerful tool to connect with industry peers, prospective employers, clients, or partners. To make the most out of LinkedIn, keep your profile up-to-date, complete with a professional photo, compelling headline, and a summary that outlines your skills and accomplishments. Think of your LinkedIn profile as your online resume and portfolio combined.

Beyond crafting a stellar profile, LinkedIn also allows you to showcase your thought leadership through its publishing platform. You can write and share articles directly on LinkedIn. This is a powerful way to demonstrate your expertise, share your insights, and provide value to your network.

Engaging with other professionals on LinkedIn doesn't have to be limited to the people you know. Consider joining LinkedIn groups that align with your industry or interests. These groups serve as discussion forums where you can share your insights, ask questions, and even find job postings. Regularly participating in these groups can help you establish a presence and build connections within your industry.

Recommendations and endorsements on LinkedIn are another way to strengthen your credibility. They serve as testimonials to your skills and expertise. Don't be shy about asking colleagues or past clients to leave you a recommendation or endorse your skills. Just remember, it's always good etiquette to return the favor.

Let's now move beyond LinkedIn. While it remains a dominant platform, others like AngelList, Xing, or GitHub offer valuable opportunities for networking within specific industries.

AngelList, for example, is a must for start-ups and those who are looking to work for them. It's an ideal platform for finding job opportunities in the start-up world, connecting with potential investors, and keeping tabs on the latest in start-up trends.

Xing is another professional networking platform that's particularly popular in Europe. It's similar to LinkedIn but has features that cater specifically to the European job market. If you're looking to expand your network across the pond, Xing is definitely worth a look.

For tech professionals, GitHub is the place to be. It's a platform where developers can collaborate on projects, contribute to open-source code, and showcase their programming prowess. By actively participating in GitHub, you can connect with other developers, learn from their code, and even catch the eye of potential employers.

Each platform comes with its own set of rules and etiquette. What works on LinkedIn might not necessarily work on AngelList or GitHub. Take some time to familiarize yourself with each platform and adjust your approach accordingly.

While it might be tempting to create a profile on every platform you come across, remember that effective networking requires time and effort. It's often more productive to pick a few platforms that align with your goals and focus your efforts there.

In the next section, we'll dive into the techniques for making authentic connections online, which is the key to effective networking on any platform. For now, know that whether it's LinkedIn or beyond, professional networking platforms are powerful tools in your digital networking arsenal. It's up to you to utilize them effectively.

Chapter 4:
Making Authentic Connections Online

Making your digital introduction is just the beginning. A meaningful business relationship blossoms from authenticity and consistent engagement. Chapter 5: Making Authentic Connections Online is designed to guide you on this journey. We delve into the etiquettes of online networking that will help you stand out in the crowd. We explore ways to establish trust and credibility, vital for fostering genuine connections in a virtual space. Finally, we demystify the art of digital conversation, teaching you to communicate effectively, stimulate engaging discussions, and listen actively to others. By mastering these elements, you'll be equipped to cultivate rich, authentic relationships that go beyond the digital handshake.

Etiquettes of Online Networking

Polished decorum and an understanding of digital norms can make a world of difference in the virtual networking space. Your digital footprint, be it comments, messages, or posts, all carry a lot of weight and form the basis of your online reputation. Therefore, it's essential to adopt an appropriate etiquette to foster effective online networking.

First and foremost, remember that although you're interacting in a digital domain, the person on the other side of the screen is very much human. Respect and courtesy are not outdated concepts but the bedrock of any interaction, including digital. Treat others the way you'd want to be treated, acknowledge their thoughts, and express your views politely. Be mindful of different time zones when you're sending a message. Don't expect immediate responses, and be patient.

When it comes to sharing and consuming content, be considerate and thoughtful. Acknowledge the source when sharing someone else's content and, when commenting, contribute positively or constructively to the discussion. You want to be a participant who adds value to conversations, not just someone who watches from the sidelines.

Professionalism and personalization should go hand in hand in online interactions. Maintain a professional tone but don't lose your personal touch. The way you phrase your messages, the kind of content you share, and how you engage with others can reflect your unique style while also maintaining a level of professionalism.

Next up is responding to others. Whether it's a comment, a private message, or a connection request, ensure you respond in a timely manner. Ignoring or delaying responses can send a signal of disinterest or negligence, neither of which benefits your networking goals. If a response requires more time, acknowledge the message and communicate when you will be able to provide a more complete response.

Just as in-person networking involves knowing when to talk, online networking requires knowing when to type. Don't dominate every conversation. Remember, networking is not a monologue but a dialogue. Leave room for others to share their thoughts and engage in what they say.

The last but crucial etiquette is about personal boundaries. It's important to respect the personal space of others even in the virtual world. Avoid oversharing and refrain from asking overly personal questions unless the other person has opened up the topic. Respect privacy settings and do not add people to groups or tag them in posts without their permission.

Now, let's talk about disagreements. Online platforms are full of diverse opinions, and you're bound to encounter views that differ from yours. It's essential to maintain respect even in disagreement. Engage in discussions with an open mind, and remember that it's okay to agree to disagree.

Lastly, proofread your communications. Typographical errors and poor grammar can come off as careless and can potentially mar your professional image. A well-written message reflects your attention to detail and respect for the recipient.

To sum up, etiquette in online networking isn't about stiff rules or robotic interactions. It's about maintaining authenticity and respect while engaging meaningfully with others. Mastering these etiquettes can put you on the fast track to cultivating thriving relationships in the digital business world.

Establishing Trust and Credibility

Building trust and credibility in online networking is much like constructing a sturdy bridge. It takes careful planning, quality materials, and painstaking efforts, but once built, it can connect you to vast opportunities. However, keep in mind that building trust doesn't happen overnight; it's a process that requires patience and consistency.

To begin, your online presence should mirror your professional persona. Your digital profile isn't just a resume; it's a showcase of your skills, knowledge, and values. From your profile picture to your professional summary and portfolio, everything should align with the image you wish to project. Be transparent, genuine, and consistent across platforms.

Sharing valuable content consistently is another way to build credibility. You become a trusted resource when you regularly provide relevant, accurate, and helpful content that benefits your network. It doesn't always have to be self-created content; even curated resources can position you as a thought leader in your field. Be consistent, but avoid overwhelming your network with too much information.

In the world of online networking, your credibility is closely tied to your interaction with others. Be responsive to messages, comments, and connection requests in a timely manner. Prompt and thoughtful responses show your commitment and respect for others' time and effort. Avoid default or automated responses, and try to add a personal touch whenever possible.

Engage with your connections by joining discussions, asking meaningful questions, and contributing your insights. It's not enough to just post content and expect trust to build on its own. You need to foster and engage in conversations, highlighting your knowledge and understanding on various topics.

Endorsements and testimonials can significantly bolster your credibility. When others vouch for your skills and competencies, it adds an external validation to your claims. Similarly, endorsing others can strengthen your relationships, demonstrate your willingness to support others, and can often be reciprocated.

Being reliable is another fundamental aspect of establishing trust. If you promise to do something - whether it's sharing a resource, making an introduction, or providing feedback - ensure you follow through. People trust those who keep their word and display integrity in their actions.

Recognize and credit the achievements and contributions of others. This not only enhances your relationships but also demonstrates your appreciation for others' expertise and knowledge. When you uplift others, it strengthens the trust between you and your network.

Privacy and confidentiality are crucial to building trust. Respect the information that others share with you and refrain from sharing it without permission. Be mindful of the privacy settings on different platforms and ensure your use of these platforms aligns with the accepted privacy norms.

Finally, always maintain a professional demeanor. Even though the lines between personal and professional can blur online, maintaining professionalism in your interactions is crucial for preserving trust and credibility. This doesn't mean you can't show your personality or have a bit of fun, but keep the context and platform in mind.

In conclusion, trust and credibility are not mere buzzwords, but foundational pillars in your online networking journey. Your authenticity, consistency, and respect for others are your most effective tools in this endeavor. So, strive to be a trusted professional others can rely on, and you'll see your digital bridges connecting you to endless possibilities.

The Art of Digital Conversation

Mastering the art of digital conversation is like learning a new language. In this vibrant landscape of emojis, memes, and hashtags, conveying a clear and impactful message can sometimes feel like navigating a labyrinth. But fret not, because mastering this art, while essential, is within everyone's reach. Here's how.

In the realm of digital conversation, clarity and conciseness reign supreme. Given the constant information bombardment everyone faces, a succinct and clear message stands a better chance of catching attention. Try to get your point across with as few words as possible, but without compromising clarity.

Grammar and punctuation are the unsung heroes of digital communication. A well-placed comma or an appropriately used exclamation mark can make all the difference in conveying your tone and intention. Embrace these tools to ensure your message is not only understood but also felt in the way you intend.

Empathy forms the bedrock of all meaningful conversations, digital or otherwise. Recognize and respect the feelings and perspectives of others, even if they differ from your own. Use empathetic language that makes your conversational partner feel seen, heard, and understood.

Effective digital conversation isn't just about broadcasting your message; it's also about active listening, or in this case, reading. Pay attention to the details in the messages you receive and respond to them in a thoughtful manner. A little reflection goes a long way in showing that you value the interaction.

Emojis, GIFs, and memes have become the new body language of digital conversations. These playful tools can help convey emotions, provide context, and add a dash of fun to the conversation. However, remember to use them judiciously and appropriately based on the nature of the relationship and platform.

When it comes to online networking, being responsive is key. Swift replies demonstrate your engagement and respect for the other person's time. However, this doesn't mean you should sacrifice thoughtfulness for speed. A prompt, well-considered response always trumps a hasty, ill-conceived one.

Context, like in any communication, plays a pivotal role in digital conversations. The norms and expectations of conversation can vary across different platforms. What works on a casual platform like Instagram might not be appropriate for a professional networking site like LinkedIn. Be mindful of the platform's conventions and adjust your communication style accordingly.

The digital world also offers unique opportunities to enhance conversations, such as the use of visuals. Including relevant images, infographics, or videos can make your messages more engaging and memorable. They can also help explain complex ideas in a more digestible manner.

Just like in real life, respect and politeness are crucial in digital interactions. Even in the face of disagreement or criticism, maintaining a level of respect can keep the conversation productive and prevent potential escalations. After all, behind every screen is a human being with feelings and dignity.

Finally, authenticity should be your guiding star. Be true to yourself in your digital conversations. Authenticity resonates with people and forms the basis for genuine connections. Remember, you're not merely exchanging words or emojis, you're sharing a part of who you are.

In conclusion, the art of digital conversation is about leveraging the unique aspects of digital platforms to communicate effectively and authentically. By applying these principles, you can turn digital conversations into meaningful connections and open doors to a world of opportunities.

PART III:
DEVELOPING
BUSINESS
RELATIONSHIPS

Chapter 5: Nurturing Online Relationships

Navigating the realm of online networking is akin to planting a seed. To help it sprout and grow, you'll need to nourish it with regular care and attention. In this chapter, we will explore the different facets of nurturing online relationships. We will delve into the importance of regular interaction and engagement, the role of collaborative digital tools for connection, and the increasingly important place webinars and virtual meetings hold in our digital world. By understanding these elements, you'll be well-equipped to cultivate thriving relationships online that could bloom into fruitful professional partnerships.

Regular Interaction and Engagement

Let's begin this journey by remembering that in the digital age, consistency is the secret sauce that binds your online networking efforts together. Regular interaction and engagement aren't just best practices; they're integral components of nurturing and maintaining online relationships.

Building business relationships online is like tending a digital garden. You can't just plant seeds (or in this case, make connections) and walk away, hoping for them to grow. These relationships require consistent attention and engagement. Whether it's responding to a message or sharing your connection's post, each interaction contributes to the growth of the relationship.

We are in an era where our digital actions translate into our virtual personalities. Therefore, frequent, meaningful interactions can lead to a robust online presence that encourages others to engage with you. You should strive to be active and visible on your chosen platforms regularly, showing up on feeds and in conversations. By maintaining a steady online presence, you're more likely to stay top-of-mind for your connections, opening up opportunities for collaboration and growth.

When we talk about engagement, it's more than just about frequency. Quality, context-appropriate interactions are critical. A 'like' or emoji reaction can suffice in some situations, but taking the time to provide thoughtful, relevant responses shows a deeper level of engagement. This depth is what strengthens connections and sets the foundation for trust and mutual respect.

Sharing content that resonates with your audience and aligns with your brand can also stimulate interaction and engagement. Content could be articles, posts, videos, or webinars that you've found useful, or original content that you've created. Content sharing is a two-way street; when you share useful content, you provide value to your connections and promote a culture of sharing within your network.

Moreover, engage with the content shared by your connections. This reciprocal exchange not only fosters a sense of community but also enriches your knowledge base. In the digital world, everyone can bring something new to the table, and embracing this collective wisdom can lead to exponential growth.

Engaging in online groups or forums related to your industry or areas of interest can also provide additional opportunities for interaction. Participating in these spaces allows you to learn from others, share your insights, and become part of a digital community.

Also, remember that feedback is a gift. When your connections comment on your posts or share their viewpoints, acknowledge their contributions. This recognition reinforces a positive interaction cycle and encourages future engagement. By being open to feedback and discussions, you create an inviting digital environment.

However, there is a fine line between being engaged and being intrusive. Respecting digital boundaries is crucial. Understand the etiquette of each platform and pay attention to cues from your connections about their comfort level with frequency and types of interactions.

Nurturing online relationships through regular interaction and engagement is a journey rather than a destination. There will be continuous learning and adjusting along the way. But with a genuine interest in your connections and a commitment to consistency, your digital garden will thrive.

Collaborative Digital Tools for Connection

In this dynamic digital age, collaboration is no longer bound by geographical locations or time zones. Thanks to the myriad of digital tools at our disposal, we can connect, collaborate, and create value with others no matter where they are. These tools offer diverse ways to engage with your network and can play a significant role in nurturing and strengthening online relationships.

Starting with the essentials, email remains an important digital tool for connection. While considered old school by some, it still serves as a reliable platform for direct and personal communication. Email is especially useful for detailed conversations, formal communication, and information that needs to be archived or referred back to later.

In contrast to the one-on-one communication offered by email, social media platforms facilitate networking on a larger scale. Tools like LinkedIn, Twitter, Facebook, and Instagram allow you to engage with a broad audience, share content, and participate in discussions. Different platforms cater to different kinds of interactions, so choosing the right one based on your objectives is critical.

Project management tools like Trello, Asana, and Basecamp are also becoming essential for online collaborations. They provide an organized space where you and your connections can manage tasks, share progress, and discuss ideas in real-time. These tools are particularly beneficial when working on shared projects or goals.

For real-time communication, instant messaging tools like Slack or Microsoft Teams have become commonplace in many professional settings. These platforms facilitate quick exchanges, reducing the time lag often associated with emails. They're also great for maintaining regular contact and fostering a sense of camaraderie with your connections.

Meanwhile, video conferencing tools like Zoom, Google Meet, or Microsoft Teams can simulate in-person meetings to a great extent. They allow for face-to-face interaction, making conversations more personal and engaging. They're perfect for in-depth discussions, brainstorming sessions, or simply catching up with your connections.

File sharing and collaborative document platforms like Google Drive or Dropbox are also incredibly useful for collaboration. These platforms allow multiple people to view, edit, and comment on documents simultaneously, making them great for team projects, brainstorming, or getting feedback.

When it comes to brainstorming and idea generation, digital whiteboards like Miro or MURAL can be game-changers. They provide a visual space for you and your connections to collaborate creatively, almost as if you were in the same room.

While these digital tools can enhance online collaboration, they should be used thoughtfully. Each tool has its strengths, and the key is to choose the ones that best serve your goals and those of your connections. Also, while technology can facilitate interaction, the real connection happens through the thoughtful and respectful way you engage with others.

Finally, remember that while digital tools are great for facilitating connections, they're merely tools. The real magic lies in the genuine interest and effort you put into nurturing these relationships. With the right balance of digital tools and authentic engagement, you'll be well on your way to building strong and lasting online relationships.

The Role of Webinars and Virtual Meetings

In the digital age, webinars and virtual meetings have emerged as powerful tools for establishing and nurturing business relationships. They have transformed how we network, allowing us to connect with a global audience from the comfort of our own homes or offices.

Webinars, or online seminars, are an effective tool for sharing knowledge, showcasing expertise, and building credibility. A well-planned and executed webinar can attract a diverse group of participants interested in the topic you're presenting. This audience is a potential network of connections who already have an interest in what you offer.

By offering value through your webinars, you give potential connections a glimpse of your knowledge and skills. It positions you as a thought leader in your field, making others more inclined to connect and collaborate with you. Furthermore, webinars offer an excellent opportunity for follow-up. By reaching out to attendees after the webinar, you can engage in deeper discussions, answer further questions, and start to build a connection.

Virtual meetings, on the other hand, offer a platform for more intimate and direct interactions. These can be one-on-one meetings or group conferences, depending on the purpose. Virtual meetings are a perfect tool for discussions, brainstorming sessions, and collaborations, providing a space for real-time interaction and communication.

In the digital business world, virtual meetings have replaced the traditional boardroom. Tools such as Zoom, Google Meet, or Microsoft Teams provide features like screen sharing, whiteboarding, and breakout rooms that enhance the collaborative experience. These meetings help nurture relationships by providing regular touchpoints where you can interact and engage with your connections.

One significant advantage of virtual meetings is the ability to record sessions. These recordings can be referred back to for clarity, used as a reference for those who couldn't attend, or repurposed into other content forms. This increases the value you get from each meeting and allows for continued engagement even after the meeting ends.

Both webinars and virtual meetings can be highly interactive, offering opportunities for participants to engage, ask questions, and provide feedback. This two-way interaction helps foster a sense of community, making participants feel seen, heard, and valued. It creates an environment of mutual learning and growth, which is a solid foundation for any business relationship.

However, as with all digital interactions, it's important to approach webinars and virtual meetings with thoughtfulness and intention. Ensure your webinars provide value and aren't just a sales pitch. For virtual meetings, respect the participants' time by sticking to the agenda and keeping the discussion focused.

It's also essential to be mindful of "Zoom fatigue" – the exhaustion that comes from too many virtual meetings. While virtual interactions are invaluable, try to balance them with asynchronous communication methods like email or instant messaging.

Overall, webinars and virtual meetings are powerful tools for building and nurturing online relationships. By providing value, fostering interaction, and approaching each webinar or meeting with respect and authenticity, you can cultivate robust and lasting business relationships in the digital age.

Chapter 6: Overcoming Challenges in Online Networking

Online networking, with all its numerous advantages, comes with its fair share of challenges. In this chapter, we'll navigate the hurdles you may encounter in the digital networking space and offer practical solutions. We'll explore strategies to manage digital fatigue, maintain a balance between professionalism and personality in online interactions, and ensure privacy and security. By confronting these challenges head-on, you'll be equipped to build healthier and more sustainable business relationships in the digital world.

Managing Digital Fatigue

It's an all too familiar scene: you've been staring at a screen for what feels like hours, the glow of the monitor beginning to take its toll. Your brain feels like it's caught in a fog and your eyes are heavy with exhaustion. This, my friends, is digital fatigue, and it's a common side effect of our increasingly online lives. As we rely more and more on digital platforms for our professional relationships, it's essential to recognize the signs of digital fatigue and take steps to manage it effectively.

The first key to managing digital fatigue is awareness. Recognize the symptoms – headaches, blurred vision, difficulty concentrating, or a general sense of being overwhelmed. The minute you start feeling any of these symptoms, it's a signal that you need to take a break. But remember, it's better to act proactively than reactively. Setting regular breaks and following them religiously is your best line of defense.

The Pomodoro Technique, a time management method developed by Francesco Cirillo, is an excellent approach to avoiding digital fatigue. The method involves breaking your work into 25-minute intervals (called "Pomodoros") separated by five-minute breaks. After completing four Pomodoros, you take a longer break of 15 to 20 minutes. This technique not only prevents digital fatigue but also boosts productivity by keeping your mind sharp and focused.

Mindful screen time is also a vital part of managing digital fatigue. Consider the necessity of each digital interaction. Does this meeting need to be a video call, or would an email suffice? Could this networking event be just as effective as a podcast or webinar that you can listen to on the go? Prioritize face-to-face interactions for essential communications and consider asynchronous communication methods for less urgent matters.

Next, ensure your workspace is ergonomically set up to reduce strain on your body. An improper workstation setup can exacerbate digital fatigue. Your screen should be at eye level, about an arm's length away. Use a chair that supports your lower back and keep your feet flat on the floor. If possible, use a separate keyboard and mouse to keep your wrists in a neutral position.

Adjusting the settings on your digital devices can also help. Most devices now offer "night mode" or "warm light" options, reducing the amount of blue light emitted by the screen. Blue light can interfere with sleep patterns and cause eye strain, so using these modes, especially in the evening, can help mitigate digital fatigue.

Regular physical activity is another crucial factor. Long periods of inactivity coupled with constant screen time can drain your energy levels. Simple exercises like stretching or going for a short walk can refresh your mind and body, combating digital fatigue. Remember, even a short burst of physical activity can go a long way in keeping you energized and focused.

Lastly, practice digital detoxing periodically. Dedicate certain hours of the day or specific days of the week to disconnect from digital devices completely. This practice not only gives your mind a break but also allows you to engage more deeply with the non-digital world around you, which can be a refreshing change of pace.

In conclusion, managing digital fatigue is all about balance. As we navigate the digital world for business networking, it's important to remember that we are humans, not machines. Incorporating these strategies into your digital networking approach will help you maintain your energy, focus, and most importantly, your health, as you build and sustain your online business relationships.

Balancing Professionalism and Personality Online

Striking the right balance between professionalism and personality online can feel like tightrope walking. Lean too much one way, and you risk coming off as impersonal and robotic. Tip too much the other way, and you might lose credibility. In the world of digital business networking, how you present yourself online matters enormously. But fear not - by following a few key strategies, you can strike a perfect balance between authenticity and professionalism.

Firstly, the content you share on your professional networking profiles should represent a healthy mix of business-related posts and personal insights. Of course, it's critical to share industry news, updates about your company, and insights into your area of expertise. However, do not hesitate to sprinkle in some personal posts to give a glimpse into your world outside of work, whether it's your hobbies, a captivating book you've recently read, or your take on a popular industry podcast. The idea is to convey that behind the professional facade, there's a relatable human being.

Secondly, always remember to keep your tone professional yet accessible. This can be a tricky balance to strike. Too much formality can make you seem unapproachable, while too much casualness might come across as unprofessional. Aim for a conversational tone. You want your connections to feel like they're having a real dialogue with you, not reading a corporate memo.

Visuals play a big part in your online presentation. Select professional photos that are high quality and properly lit. However, don't let that professionalism make your photos look staged or unapproachable. Your profile photo, for instance, should not only show that you're a competent professional but also hint at your personality. Are you adventurous? A photo from a hiking trip could work. Love painting? Why not a photo in your art studio? These visuals subtly tell your story beyond your job title.

When it comes to engaging with others online, remember to be courteous and professional, but don't shy away from showcasing your personality. In discussions and conversations, express your opinions honestly but respectfully. Remember that people are more likely to engage with those who appear open, considerate, and genuine.

Your online biography or 'About Me' section is a perfect place to integrate your professionalism and personality. Start by detailing your qualifications, professional achievements, and areas of expertise. Then, segue into more personal information - perhaps you could mention where you're from, your love for cooking or the fact that you're learning a new language. This blend of professional and personal details makes for a well-rounded introduction.

Language and communication style are another way to balance professionalism and personality. While it's necessary to maintain correct grammar and avoid slang or colloquial language, don't hesitate to use a conversational and friendly tone. The goal is to sound like a real person, not an automated response system.

It's also important to respond to comments and engage with posts from your connections. Engaging does not only mean liking or giving a cursory response but offering thoughtful comments, starting meaningful conversations, and showing interest in what others are saying. This approach not only shows your professionalism but also your personality and your genuine interest in building relationships.

Understanding your audience also helps strike the right balance. The content, tone, and style that works for one platform or group might not work for another. Always tailor your approach based on who you're interacting with and the platform you're using.

Lastly, be consistent. Once you've found that sweet spot between professionalism and personality, stick with it. Consistency helps people know what to expect from you and fosters trust, a key element in building solid online business relationships.

To sum up, balancing professionalism and personality online isn't an exact science - it requires constant adjustment and calibration. But with practice and intent, you can create a compelling online persona that not only attracts professional opportunities but also allows for genuine connections in the digital networking world.

Ensuring Privacy and Security in Online Interactions

Privacy and security are fundamental when it comes to navigating the digital realm, especially in online business networking. When you're sharing information and connecting with people across multiple platforms, it's essential to take measures that protect both your personal data and the data of others. This section will guide you through some key steps to ensure your online interactions remain safe and private.

The first step is understanding your privacy settings. Every social and professional networking platform has privacy settings that control who can see your content, how people can search for you, and who can send you requests or messages. Take the time to explore these settings and customize them to your comfort level. Be mindful of what you're sharing and with whom you're sharing.

When it comes to personal information, less is more. You don't need to disclose every detail about your life or work. Share only the information that serves your networking goals. Be cautious with sensitive information such as your home address, personal phone number, or financial information. This not only helps protect you from potential security threats but also maintains a level of professional boundary.

Never underestimate the importance of a strong password. It's your first line of defense against hackers and data breaches. Make sure your password is a combination of letters, numbers, and symbols. Avoid using easily guessed information like your birthdate, name, or simple sequences. Use a different password for each platform and consider using a reputable password manager.

Remember, your digital interactions are not limited to what you post or share; they also include your responses to others. Be cautious about clicking on links or downloading files from unfamiliar sources. Cybercriminals often use these methods to install malware or gain access to your data. If something seems off or too good to be true, it probably is.

Be cautious when connecting with people you don't know. While the purpose of online networking is to make new connections, not everyone has good intentions. If a profile looks suspicious or if someone is excessively eager to know more about you, trust your instincts and maintain your distance.

Ensure your devices are secure. Keep your computer, smartphone, and other devices that you use for networking up to date with the latest software and security patches. Consider installing a reputable security software solution that includes antivirus and firewall protection. These measures add another layer of defense against potential cyber threats.

If you're participating in online meetings or webinars, ensure the platform used is secure and provides end-to-end encryption. Be mindful of what is visible in your video background. Accidentally revealing sensitive information can lead to privacy issues. Also, it's good practice to mute your microphone when not speaking to avoid unintentional background disclosures.

Another aspect to consider is the data that social media platforms collect about you. Familiarize yourself with the terms of service and privacy policies of the platforms you use. While they can be dense and filled with jargon, understanding them can help you make informed decisions about your privacy settings and how you interact on the platform.

Lastly, it's worth noting that privacy and security are ongoing concerns. Regularly review your privacy settings, check your posts, and be aware of the latest scams or threats in the digital world. Just as you'd periodically assess your professional progress or update your goals, your online security needs regular attention and care.

In conclusion, while the digital world offers enormous potential for networking and growing your business relationships, it also brings challenges in privacy and security. By being proactive and diligent, you can ensure your online interactions remain both productive and safe.

PART IV: MAINTAINING BUSINESS RELATIONSHIPS

Chapter 7:
Long-term Relationships in a Fast-Paced Digital World

In this dynamic, high-speed digital era, it's crucial not just to create and develop business relationships, but to sustain them over the long haul. This chapter shines a light on this crucial aspect of digital networking. We'll delve into strategies to keep your network engaged over time, show you how to tailor and customize your interactions for more significant impact, and guide you in adapting to ever-changing digital trends. By investing your time and effort in these areas, you'll find it's possible to cultivate enduring business relationships that stand the test of time, despite the fast pace of the digital world.

Sustaining Engagement Over Time

Cultivating relationships is not a one-time event but rather a continual effort to engage and connect. Building trust and forming meaningful bonds in the digital realm requires more than the initial outreach; it necessitates consistent, value-adding engagement over time. Let's unpack some strategies that can help you maintain this momentum and keep your connections alive and thriving.

The first step towards sustaining engagement is understanding that relationships evolve. It's essential to be flexible and adaptive to the changes that occur in professional relations. This flexibility can manifest itself as altering communication styles, adapting to new platforms, or simply adjusting to the varying demands on your connection's time and attention. Being able to navigate these changes seamlessly is integral to maintaining long-term engagement.

Content sharing is a powerful strategy to sustain engagement. By sharing relevant content – be it articles, videos, or industry insights – you add value to your network. This not only gives them a reason to engage with you but also positions you as a resourceful connection. However, it's crucial to ensure that the content you share aligns with your connections' interests and professional needs.

Creating opportunities for interaction is another way to maintain engagement. Regular check-ins, wishing them on significant occasions, or inviting them to webinars or events where they might gain some value helps to keep the relationship active. This way, you are not just another connection on their list but someone they regularly interact with.

One must not underestimate the power of responsiveness in digital communication. Being prompt in responding to messages, comments, or emails makes the other person feel valued. Remember, digital conversations, much like their offline counterparts, are built on mutual interaction. Your responsiveness encourages the same from your connections.

In an age where personal branding has taken the center stage, maintaining a consistent and engaging online presence is vital. Regularly updating your social media profiles, sharing your achievements and projects, and participating in discussions related to your field can keep your connections engaged. They're more likely to interact with an active profile than one that seems stagnant.

Remember, your aim is to be a connection that adds value. Be the one who shares the latest industry news, initiates thought-provoking discussions, and supports others' posts with likes, comments, and shares. These actions show that you're not only active in the digital space but also invested in your network's growth and success.

In the digital world, personalization is key. People appreciate when they are addressed by their names and when the content shared with them resonates with their interests or needs. Whenever possible, customize your communication to make your connections feel special and seen.

While focusing on engagement, it's important to respect boundaries. We all have experienced the annoyance of being spammed with messages or tagged in irrelevant posts. Excessive communication can lead to connection fatigue, the exact opposite of your goal.

Also, understand that not every interaction needs to be strictly professional. Shared hobbies, interests, or experiences can foster more profound connections. Don't shy away from discussing these, as they can add another layer of depth to your professional relationships.

Finally, patience and persistence are your allies. Building relationships takes time and continuous effort. Stay patient and keep engaging consistently, without expecting immediate returns. Over time, these small interactions build up, leading to more robust and enduring relationships.

In summary, sustaining engagement over time in a digital world is an art. By offering value, maintaining consistent communication, respecting boundaries, and showing persistence, you can keep your business relationships healthy, thriving, and mutually beneficial.

Personalizing and Customizing Your Interactions

The digital landscape offers a unique opportunity to personalize and customize your interactions, which is vital for building lasting, meaningful relationships. This approach moves beyond the cookie-cutter networking strategies and helps you connect on a more profound, individual level. Let's delve into how you can make your interactions more personalized and tailored to each connection.

To personalize your interactions, you must first know your connections. In the digital space, this means researching their online presence. Look into their interests, their work, their posts, and the things they engage with online. This information can give you insights into what they value and how you can communicate in a way that resonates with them.

Equipped with this understanding, you can tailor your communication. If someone shares articles about sustainability in business, for example, you might reach out to them with a recent study on the topic. By doing so, you demonstrate that you've taken the time to understand their interests and are offering them something of value.

Remember to keep your interactions human and authentic. While it's a digital space, there's a real person behind each profile. Avoid sounding like a generic marketing message or a corporate bot. Show your personality and address your connections in a genuine, friendly tone. Use their name, refer to previous conversations or shared experiences – this creates a sense of familiarity and warmth.

Consider also the platform you're using for communication. Different platforms have different cultures and standards. A message on LinkedIn might be more formal and professional, while on Twitter, you could afford to be a bit more casual and concise. Tailoring your interaction style to the platform can help you resonate better with your connections.

Language plays a crucial role in personalizing interactions. If your connection uses a certain kind of language – maybe they're more formal or perhaps they love using emojis – mirror that to some extent in your responses. This is called linguistic matching, and it can subtly make your communication feel more aligned and congenial.

Timeliness is another aspect of customization. Wishing someone on their work anniversary or the launch of their new project can make your connection feel valued. However, remember to add a personal touch to these messages. Don't just rely on LinkedIn's automated message prompts. Personalizing these interactions shows you genuinely care and aren't just ticking a networking box.

Personalization also extends to the type of content you share or tag people in. If you come across an article or event that you believe would be beneficial to a connection, share it with them. Again, this shows that you're thinking of their interests and are actively contributing to their professional development.

One word of caution: while personalization is important, it's equally crucial to respect the other person's privacy. Personalization should be based on publicly available information and shared within the context of your professional relationship. Avoid anything that might come off as intrusive or inappropriate.

Finally, don't forget that personalization is a two-way street. Encourage your connections to share, engage, and communicate in a way that's most comfortable and authentic for them. This reciprocal personalization strengthens your bonds and makes for more meaningful interactions.

In conclusion, personalizing and customizing your interactions are potent tools in your digital networking arsenal. By taking a more tailored, human-centered approach, you can foster deeper connections and turn your digital handshakes into enduring professional relationships.

Dealing with Changes in Digital Trends

The digital landscape is dynamic and rapidly changing. New platforms emerge, user preferences shift, and technologies advance at an unprecedented pace. Keeping up with these changes and adapting your strategies accordingly is crucial to maintaining robust online relationships and expanding your digital network. This section will provide insights on how you can effectively deal with changes in digital trends.

Being informed is the first step towards managing changes in digital trends. Stay updated on the latest trends, technologies, and platforms relevant to your field and networking. Subscribe to newsletters, follow thought leaders, and participate in online communities where you can stay informed about the shifting digital landscape.

Next, adopt a mindset of continuous learning. The pace of change in the digital world requires constant upskilling and reskilling. Embrace new technologies and platforms as they emerge and learn how they can be utilized for networking and building relationships.

Keep your online presence adaptable. As new trends emerge, it may be necessary to adjust your online presence to stay relevant. This could mean revamping your LinkedIn profile, rebranding your personal website, or jumping onto a new social media platform. But remember, always prioritize quality over quantity. It's better to have a strong, active presence on a few platforms than a weak, inactive one across many.

Understand that not every trend is relevant for you or your network. While it's essential to be aware of what's happening, you don't need to jump onto every passing trend. Be selective and assess the potential value of a new tool or platform before investing your time and effort into it.

One significant trend to look out for is the rise of video-based platforms. With the surge in popularity of platforms like TikTok and Instagram Reels, the way people consume content is changing. Learning to create engaging video content could be a valuable skill for networking in this new digital landscape.

As you adjust to new trends, remember to keep your connections at the forefront. If a new trend helps you provide more value to your network or engage with them more effectively, it's worth considering. If not, feel free to let it pass by.

Maintaining your digital security is paramount when dealing with changes in digital trends. New platforms or tools often come with new security risks. Always research and understand these potential risks before diving in.

Another crucial aspect of dealing with changes is flexibility. Be prepared to adjust your strategies as needed. If you find a platform is no longer serving your networking goals, or your network is shifting to another platform, be ready to adapt.

Embrace the unique benefits that come with each new trend. Each new tool or platform comes with its unique set of features and benefits. Look for ways to leverage these to build and maintain your relationships.

Finally, as you navigate these changes, remember the core principles of networking remain the same. Despite the ever-changing landscape, the essence of networking – building authentic, reciprocal relationships – remains constant.

To sum it up, dealing with changes in digital trends is a key aspect of digital networking. By staying informed, being adaptable, and maintaining a focus on your relationships, you can navigate these changes effectively and continue to grow your network in the digital age.

Chapter 8: Turning Connections into Collaborations

After all the work of forging online connections, creating credibility, and maintaining engagement, the real magic comes when we transform these digital connections into meaningful collaborations. Chapter 9 will delve into the process of transitioning from networking to collaborating in the digital age, starting with strategies for leveraging online networking for business opportunities. We'll then move on to explore how digital tools facilitate collaboration, whether it's cloud-based workspaces or innovative communication tools. Finally, we'll investigate real-life case studies that exemplify successful digital collaborations, showcasing the potential of what can be achieved when digital connections are turned into collaborations.

Leveraging Online Networking for Business Opportunities

In the interconnected digital landscape, the lines between networking and opportunity generation often blur. With every interaction, every post, every conversation, you are positioning yourself within a complex web of potential business ventures. To successfully leverage online networking for business opportunities, you need to approach each interaction with intentionality, understanding that each digital handshake can lead to a wealth of possibilities.

Begin by being strategic about the content you share. Each piece of content should subtly reflect your professional skills, business values, and unique selling propositions. This doesn't mean every post should be a sales pitch—far from it! Instead, you want to use your content to showcase your expertise, demonstrate your values, and subtly indicate what you bring to the table. Think of your content as your digital elevator pitch.

The second step is to be proactive in reaching out and forging connections. Don't just wait for opportunities to come to you. If you come across someone on LinkedIn who seems to share your values and goals, send them a personalized connection request. Join industry-related groups on Facebook or Slack and engage in the discussions there. The more active you are, the more visible you become.

Furthermore, in the realm of digital networking, alliances can be a significant force multiplier. Partner with individuals or organizations that complement your own. These collaborations allow you to extend your reach, tap into new networks, and amplify your influence. Joint webinars, co-authored blog posts, or cross-promotions on social media can serve as platforms for these partnerships.

To leverage networking effectively, you must also become comfortable with the direct approach. When you come across a promising connection, don't hesitate to explore the potential of a collaboration. This might mean proposing a joint project, suggesting a partnership, or even asking outright for a job opportunity. Remember, the worst that can happen is they'll say no.

Remember that networking doesn't end with the initial connection. Nurturing these relationships is critical for transforming networking efforts into business opportunities.

Regularly engage with your network's content, contribute to discussions, and provide value wherever possible. This not only keeps you on their radar but also positions you as an active, engaged, and valuable member of their digital community.

Lastly, don't limit your efforts to professional networking sites like LinkedIn. Remember that opportunities can come from the most unlikely places. From Twitter threads to Instagram comments, potential business opportunities can be anywhere. The key is to remain open, adaptable, and alert to the potential in every interaction.

So, view every tweet, every LinkedIn post, and every virtual conversation as an opportunity in disguise. The digital landscape is ripe with potential; you just have to know where to look. Be strategic, proactive, and unafraid to reach out. You might be surprised by the opportunities that come your way when you start leveraging online networking with intention.

Collaborating in the Cloud

The cloud has become a powerful tool for businesses and individuals alike, transforming how we work, communicate, and collaborate. The cloud's ability to store and share data has broken down geographical boundaries, allowing for seamless collaboration regardless of location. This makes it an invaluable tool for fostering business relationships and turning connections into collaborations.

The first step to effective cloud collaboration is choosing the right platform. Today, a variety of cloud-based collaboration tools are available, each offering unique functionalities. Google Workspace, Microsoft 365, Dropbox, and Slack are just a few examples. Your choice should be guided by the needs of your team or project. Consider factors like ease of use, integration with other tools, security features, and the type of collaboration you'll be doing.

Once you've chosen a platform, make sure everyone involved knows how to use it. A tool is only as effective as the people wielding it. Hold a training session, provide resources, or ensure that user guides are easily accessible. Familiarity with the platform will result in smoother collaboration and a more productive team.

Next, establish guidelines for how the platform will be used. Just like in a physical workspace, digital spaces require organization and management. Without a system, your cloud workspace can quickly become chaotic. Set up folders for different projects, establish naming conventions for files, and determine who has editing permissions. A little organization can go a long way in making collaborations more efficient.

However, the cloud isn't just for storing and sharing files—it's also a hub for communication. Many cloud platforms incorporate chat features, video conferencing capabilities, and project management tools. These can be used to discuss projects in real-time, hold virtual meetings, or keep track of tasks and deadlines. By centralizing communication within the cloud, you can keep all relevant information and discussions in one place.

Don't forget about the cloud's ability to facilitate co-creation. Multiple people can work on a single document simultaneously, allowing for real-time collaboration and immediate feedback. This can drastically speed up workflows and encourage more dynamic, interactive brainstorming sessions.

But, while the cloud is a powerful tool, it's essential to remember it's not a replacement for personal connection. It's a tool to facilitate collaboration, not a substitute for it. Therefore, even as you utilize the cloud, make sure to maintain personal relationships. Regularly check in with your collaborators, offer support, and celebrate successes.

Also, remember to practice and respect digital etiquette while collaborating in the cloud. This might include being responsive, respecting time zones when scheduling meetings, and giving credit where it's due. As in any professional setting, respect and courtesy are key to successful collaboration.

Security is also paramount when collaborating in the cloud. Ensure sensitive data is protected by using strong passwords, enabling two-factor authentication, and being wary of phishing attempts. Regularly backup your data to prevent loss and ensure you're using a trusted, secure cloud platform.

So, as you navigate the digital landscape and forge business relationships, don't shy away from the opportunities offered by the cloud. When leveraged effectively, the cloud can become your collaborative hub, a place where ideas merge, projects take shape, and business relationships flourish into productive collaborations.

Case Studies of Successful Digital Collaborations

When it comes to demonstrating the power of digital collaboration, there's no better way than through real-life examples. The following case studies showcase how businesses leveraged digital collaboration to not only adapt in the face of challenge, but also to thrive and innovate.

First, let's look at a case that hit global headlines: how NASA managed to run its Mars Curiosity Rover Mission with a team spread across continents. NASA used a combination of cloud-based tools, virtual reality, and digital collaboration platforms to allow its globally dispersed team to work together as if they were in the same room. The mission was a testament to the power of digital collaboration, showcasing how high-stakes, complex projects can be run successfully in a virtual environment.

Next, consider a smaller-scale, but no less inspiring, example: a start-up tech company named Zapier. As a fully remote company since its inception, Zapier has relied entirely on digital collaboration tools to function. Through cloud-based tools, it has managed to maintain strong communication, efficient workflows, and a unified company culture among a team that spans multiple time zones. It is a testament to the idea that a physical office is not a prerequisite for success.

Our third case involves a traditional business forced to evolve in the face of the pandemic: the fashion brand, Balenciaga. When the global pandemic hit and halted in-person fashion shows, the company turned to digital solutions. Balenciaga presented its Fall 2021 collection in an immersive online environment, allowing guests to explore the virtual space at their leisure. This combination of fashion and digital innovation resulted in a memorable, impactful event.

Moving on, let's consider a case from the non-profit sector: the World Wildlife Fund (WWF). As a global organization, the WWF has teams located all around the world. Through the use of digital collaboration tools, it has been able to coordinate global campaigns, share information quickly, and work together effectively despite geographical distances. It demonstrates how digital collaboration can be leveraged in service of a common goal.

Our final case takes us to the world of entertainment: the production of the animated film, "The Croods: A New Age." When the pandemic hit in early 2020, DreamWorks Animation needed to find a way to keep production going with a suddenly remote team. Using cloud-based collaboration tools and virtual private networks, they managed to successfully complete the movie remotely, showcasing how digital collaboration can be used to overcome unprecedented challenges.

These examples show us the breadth and depth of digital collaboration's potential. From space missions to fashion shows, from start-ups to non-profits, the power of digital collaboration tools is being harnessed in all sorts of contexts. As you consider how to apply the concepts of this book to your own business relationships, let these cases serve as both inspiration and validation of the power of digital collaboration.

Chapter 9: The Future of Business Relationships

As we gaze into the horizon of business relationships, it's clear that the future is already here, marked by constant evolution and innovation. In this final chapter, we'll delve into the dynamics of the swiftly shifting networking landscape, exploring how you can adapt to the inevitable digital shifts that are yet to come. We'll journey into a future where digital and physical worlds continue to merge, demanding increased adaptability and resilience. By the end, we will offer closing remarks to wrap up our exploration of digital networking, grounding us in the present while preparing for the future.

The Evolving Networking Landscape

As we move into the future, the networking landscape continues to evolve at an extraordinary pace. Technology's relentless advancement, coupled with our ever-increasing reliance on digital platforms, is constantly reshaping how we connect and collaborate with each other in the business world.

A key facet of the evolving networking landscape is the continued diversification and expansion of digital platforms. Even as stalwarts like LinkedIn, Facebook, and Twitter remain influential, new platforms continue to emerge. These platforms cater to niche markets or introduce innovative ways of interacting, such as augmented and virtual reality experiences. As a result, businesses and professionals have a broader range of channels to establish and nurture connections than ever before.

This diversity, however, comes with the challenge of fragmentation. With countless platforms vying for attention, it can become overwhelming to maintain a presence everywhere. A more strategic approach might be to identify where your target network frequents and focus your energy there. The evolving landscape demands adaptability, but also a keen sense of direction.

In parallel, the trend towards remote and digital-first workplaces is intensifying. The global events of recent years have demonstrated the viability and benefits of remote work, leading to a rise in fully remote companies and teams. This shift broadens the potential networking pool, as geographical barriers become increasingly irrelevant.

Yet, this trend also transforms networking norms. The casual chats by the water cooler or the serendipitous encounters at a physical networking event have no direct equivalent in a remote environment. Professionals and companies are innovating ways to recreate these informal networking opportunities in the digital space, leading to solutions like virtual co-working sessions or 'water cooler' channels on team communication platforms.

Privacy and security, already important concerns in the digital age, will become even more critical. As we share more about ourselves online to build connections, we also expose more data that could be misused. Businesses and individuals alike need to be vigilant about privacy settings, data sharing policies, and the latest cyber threats.

Moreover, technology's role in facilitating connections is set to grow even further. Artificial intelligence and machine learning are playing an increasingly important part in helping individuals and businesses identify potential connections and opportunities, analyze trends, and even automate parts of the networking process.

At the same time, there's a growing recognition of the value of the human touch in digital interactions. While automation can be a boon, there's a keen awareness that networking, at its heart, is about building genuine human connections. Balancing efficiency and authenticity is a key aspect of navigating the evolving networking landscape.

In the midst of these changes, the core principles of networking remain. Trust, mutual benefit, and a genuine interest in others are still at the heart of every meaningful business relationship. Even as the networking landscape evolves, the essentials that drive it stay the same.

Adapting to Future Digital Shifts

As we anticipate future changes in the digital networking landscape, adaptability becomes a critical skill. Whether it's the emergence of a new social media platform, shifts in data privacy regulations, or the introduction of novel technologies like augmented reality, adapting to these changes can make the difference between thriving in your business relationships or becoming lost in the shuffle.

The first step in adapting to future shifts is developing a mindset of continuous learning. The digital age is characterized by rapid, constant change. Being open to learning about new platforms, technologies, and trends can position you to take advantage of opportunities as they arise.

In the face of constant change, it's also vital to build a strong foundation. The nuances of each platform or technology may change, but the principles of good communication, respect, and authenticity in business relationships remain constant.

By mastering these basics, you're equipped to succeed in any digital environment.

As part of this, understanding the evolving expectations and norms of online communication is crucial. Just as face-to-face interactions have unspoken rules and etiquette, so too do digital interactions. Being aware of these norms and how they're changing can help you connect more effectively and avoid potential misunderstandings.

Another essential element in adapting to future digital shifts is cultivating a robust online presence that accurately reflects your personal or business brand. This presence should be adaptable and ready to evolve as new platforms emerge and existing ones change.

As we move into an increasingly data-driven age, learning to harness data can be a powerful way to adapt to future shifts. From tracking engagement on your social media posts to using analytics to understand your audience better, data can provide invaluable insights that drive your networking strategy.

Incorporating flexibility into your networking approach is also beneficial. This might mean being ready to experiment with new platforms or technologies, even if they're outside of your comfort zone. It could also involve being open to new ways of doing things, such as transitioning from traditional face-to-face meetings to virtual collaboration tools.

In parallel, it's crucial to stay updated on issues around digital privacy and security. As regulations evolve and cyber threats become more sophisticated, keeping your data - and that of your connections - secure is increasingly important.

Above all, adapting to future digital shifts involves an element of anticipation. By staying informed about emerging trends and understanding the broader digital landscape, you can position yourself to adapt to changes before they become mainstream.

Finally, it's worth remembering that at the heart of every business relationship is people. No matter how digital shifts reshape the networking landscape, maintaining a focus on building genuine, human connections will always serve you well.

Closing Remarks

As we wrap up our digital journey, it's time to reflect on the path we've traversed together, exploring the vast and complex landscape of networking in our modern, connected world. We've delved into history, navigated the current scene, and peeked into the future. Yet, the journey isn't over. In fact, it's only just beginning.

Building business relationships in a digital world is an ongoing process, a ceaseless effort of learning, adapting, and connecting. Like the digital environment itself, the rules and tools are ever-changing, requiring us to stay flexible and resilient. Nevertheless, certain fundamentals remain steady amid the digital flux. They are the anchors, the timeless truths of networking, irrespective of the medium.

Authenticity, trust, and respect have been the cornerstones of building meaningful relationships, whether in the physical realm or in the digital sphere. They underpin every interaction, every connection, and every collaboration. These principles have formed the backbone of our discussions and should continue to guide you as you forge ahead on your digital networking journey.

Just as vital as these core values is a commitment to continuous learning. The digital world doesn't stand still.

New technologies, platforms, and modes of communication spring up constantly. Embracing a learning mindset, keeping abreast of changes, and being ready to adapt are essential skills for the digital networker.

Remember, however, that the pursuit of learning and adaptation shouldn't lead to an overemphasis on technology itself. Technology is a means to an end, not the end itself. Keep your focus on people, not platforms. After all, networking is fundamentally about building relationships with people.

As we've explored, the digital landscape offers numerous opportunities for connection. Social media, professional platforms, digital meetings, collaborative tools—each serves as a different conduit for creating, nurturing, and sustaining business relationships. Yet, it's not enough to simply exist in these spaces; one must know how to navigate them with grace and tact, balancing professionalism with personality.

Privacy and security are another pair of constant companions in our digital journey. They are crucial considerations in every interaction and transaction. As digital networking evolves, so does the need to protect our data and respect the data of others. Understanding and respecting digital boundaries will continue to be paramount.

Finally, remember to find joy in the journey. Networking isn't merely a task or a strategy; it's a means of enriching our lives, broadening our perspectives, and fostering meaningful connections. As you engage with others in the digital realm, allow yourself to appreciate the unique opportunities for learning, growth, and connection that this incredible digital age affords us.

In conclusion, thank you for joining me on this digital voyage. May the knowledge and insights shared serve as a sturdy ship to navigate the vast and exciting ocean of digital networking. Happy sailing!

Appendix

As you set sail on your digital networking journey, this appendix is here to offer a hand in guiding you through the swirling seas of social media, collaborative tools, and various other aspects we've covered in this book. Here you'll find a compilation of resources that can aid you in building business relationships in this digital age.

List of Major Social Media Platforms and their Key Uses in Professional Networking

- *LinkedIn*: Primarily a professional networking platform, ideal for showcasing your skills, experiences, and endorsements. A place to connect with potential employers, clients, and professional peers.

- *Twitter*: A microblogging site that's excellent for staying updated on industry news and trends, engaging with thought leaders, and sharing your insights.

- *Facebook*: While often used for personal connections, it also offers Groups and Pages for professional interests, events, and community building.

- *Instagram*: A visually driven platform, best for industries where visual impact matters, like fashion, food, art, and travel. Also used for personal branding.

- *TikTok*: Known for its short, engaging videos, it can be a unique platform for creative brand storytelling and reaching a younger demographic.

List of Major Professional Platforms

- *LinkedIn*: As mentioned earlier, it is a premier professional networking site.

- *AngelList*: For startups and tech companies looking for investors, and job seekers interested in working for startups.

- *Xing*: A European professional networking site, similar to LinkedIn.

- *B2B Wave*: A B2B eCommerce platform for wholesalers, manufacturers, and distributors.

List of Collaborative Digital Tools

- *Google Workspace*: Offers a suite of productivity and collaboration tools, including Gmail, Docs, Sheets, Slides, and Meet.

- *Slack*: An instant messaging platform designed for team collaboration with the ability to create different channels for various topics.

- *Trello*: A project management tool using the Kanban system for organizing tasks and tracking progress.

- *Zoom*: A platform for video and audio conferencing, chat, and webinars.

- *Asana*: A project management tool to help teams organize, track, and manage their work.

- *Microsoft Teams*: A collaboration platform within Microsoft 365, which integrates with other MS apps.

Resources for Staying Updated with Digital Trends

- *TechCrunch*: A leading technology media property, dedicated to obsessively profiling startups, reviewing new Internet products, and breaking tech news.

- *Mashable*: A global, multi-platform media and entertainment company. Mashable is a go-to source for tech, digital culture, and entertainment content.

- *Social Media Examiner*: An online guide to the social media jungle, offering articles, news, and expert interviews covering all aspects of the social media marketing sphere.

- *Wired*: A monthly magazine that provides an in-depth coverage of current and future trends in technology.

Remember, as the digital landscape evolves, so should your resource bank. Stay curious and proactive in exploring new tools and platforms, and most importantly, happy networking!

Glossary

Algorithm: A set of rules or procedures that a computer follows to perform a specific task or solve a problem. In social media, algorithms determine what content appears in a user's feed based on their behavior and preferences.

Cloud Computing: The practice of using a network of remote servers hosted on the internet to store, manage, and process data, rather than a local server or a personal computer.

Collaborative Digital Tools: Online tools that enable people to work together on projects, even if they are not in the same physical location. These tools can include shared documents, project management applications, and communication platforms.

Digital Fatigue: A state of mental exhaustion and stress caused by overuse of digital devices or overexposure to digital information and interactions.

Digital First: A business strategy or approach that prioritizes the use of digital technologies in the delivery of services or products.

Digital Handshake: The first impression you make online, often through a social media profile, website, or digital interaction.

Hashtag: A word or phrase preceded by a hash sign (#), used on social media to identify messages on a specific topic.

LinkedIn: A social media platform designed primarily for professional networking. Users can post their career history, skills, and professional accomplishments, and can also follow companies, join industry groups, and connect with other professionals.

Microblogging: A type of blogging that allows users to post brief text updates or other content, such as photos or short videos. Twitter is a popular microblogging platform.

Networking: The act of interacting with others to exchange information and develop professional or social contacts.

Personal Branding: The process of developing a "mark" or identity that is created around your personal name or career. This "brand" can help to attract people to your business, influence others, and enhance your career.

Professional Networking: The process of creating and nurturing relationships with others in your industry or field to enhance your career, learn from others, and share information and resources.

Remote Work: A flexible working style that allows professionals to work outside of a traditional office environment. It is based on the concept that work does not need to be done in a specific place to be executed successfully.

Social Media: Websites and applications that enable users to create and share content or to participate in social networking. Popular platforms include Facebook, Instagram, Twitter, and LinkedIn.

Webinar: A live, virtual event that is executed online. It is an educational or instructive session that includes audio and visual communication between a speaker and attendees. Webinar software enables the sharing of slides and interactive participation through chat boxes and Q&A features.

Zoom: An online video communication tool used for video conferencing, webinars, and screen sharing, among other uses.

About the Author

Hannah enjoys exploring the vibrant cultural scene of Los Angeles, from its bustling food markets to its renowned art galleries. She believes in a balanced lifestyle where work, personal development, and leisure coexist harmoniously.

Hannah continues to push the boundaries in the marketing and networking world, ever motivated by her commitment to education and the sharing of knowledge. Her approach, steeped in innovation, informs her work, making "Beyond Handshakes: Building Business Relationships in a Digital World" a compelling read for anyone navigating the digital networking landscape.